WONDERFUL SWEDEN

THE GLORIOUS LANDSCAPE AND DELICIOUS CUISINE

PHOTOS: **BRUNO EHRS** TEXT: **TOMAS TENGBY** RECIPES: **KC WALLBERG**

ICA BOKFÖRLAG

LAPPLAND
DALARNA
STOCKHOLM
GOTLAND
HALLAND
SKÅNE

Join us on a culinary journey through Sweden, from Lappland up north to Skåne down south. Maybe once you have learned about the delights of Sweden on paper, you will be inspired to do it "live" next time, so that you can see and taste everything you have read about.

Or you can relive past experiences in Sweden.

A culinary and geographical journey through Sweden with glorious pictures, text and recipes. We are not covering the entire country, rather we will make six stops and offer a sampling of many different dishes.

Experience the untamed wilderness of Lappland, the summer warmth of Dalarna, the magical views of Gotland, the sea off the west coast of Halland, the unique archipelago that makes up the capital of Stockholm, and the southern charm of Skåne.

Enjoy the unique flavors of cloudberry parfait, homemade crispbread, strawberry-rhubarb soup, cod with horseradish and fresh shrimp, Skåne apple cake, pea soup, meatballs, marinated salmon, herring and much more.

Bruno Ehrs took the beautiful pictures. All the good food was prepared by Karl-Christer Wallberg. And Tomas Tengby is your guide.

We hope that you too will be ready to proclaim: Wonderful Sweden!

CONTENTS

SEGLORA CHURCH IN SKANSEN, STOCKHOLM

HALLAND

On the surface, Halland is a narrow strip of landscape. And yet, you can find kilometer-long beaches, barren rocky islets, fertile plains and dense forests here – and all that is mirrored in the cuisine.

Halland, in southwestern Sweden, is bordered by Skåne, Småland and Bohuslän. Archaeological finds indicate that there have been settlements here since the end of the Ice Age.

Early on, perhaps as early as the sixth century, Halland was part of the area which eventually became Denmark. When Denmark was unified in Viking times, Halland was included. Denmark, Norway and Sweden fought for control of this landscape over many centuries. During the 14th century, Halland changed its nationality 10 times in 60 years.

The worst period for the people of Halland was from the middle of the 16th to the beginning of the 18th century, when the area was the site of many battles between Sweden and Denmark. All that war bled Halland in many ways and left the region in poverty.

Since 1645, Halland has been Swedish. In other words, Halland was Danish for longer than it has been Swedish.

There are three types of landscape in Halland, going from west to east: coast, plains and forest. The coast is considered the Swedish Riviera, with kilometers of sandy beaches in Tylösand, unique seaside moors, rocky archipelago, small fishing villages, fertile plains, cultivated rolling hills, lakes, pure wilderness and great, dense forests.

You can find everything you need to eat and live well here, but at the end of the 19th century, failed harvests turned Halland into a barren landscape with near famine conditions. For that reason, Halland had the highest emigration in percentage of population to the US.

Today, this landscape is often associated with food. Statistics also indicate that people live well here. Average number of workdays lost through illness is lower than in the rest of Sweden, and the average lifespan has been one of the highest in the country and in the world since the early 1900s.

LEFT: BUA LIGHTHOUSE. **NEXT SPREAD:** PICTURES FROM THE COAST OF HALLAND (BUA, GETTERÖN ISLAND AND TYLÖSAND).

THE WEATHER VANE AT THE VARBERG OPEN-AIR BATH HOUSE,
REMAINING PICTURES FROM BUA.

Whenever anyone asks about typical Halland food, three favorites are always mentioned: Kale, salmon and horseradish.

No Halland Christmas table is complete without kale cooked in ham broth or bouillon and later sautéed in butter and finished off with cream.

There has always been salmon, and there was so much of it in days of old, that it was served once a day on the farms. Sometimes workers demanded one salmon-free day a week in their contracts. The salmon is also "patron of the landscape" in Halland.

Halland is now Sweden's leading producer of horseradish.

But Halland food is so much more than just these three ingredients. The forests provide deer, moose, roedeer, berries and mushrooms. The plains provide vegetables, grains, meat and cheeses. And the coast provides fish and shellfish.

In this dish, we cover two kinds of landscape with cod and shrimp from the ocean and horseradish, eggs, potatoes and dill from the plains.

And those who have sampled fish around the globe will attest that standards are high in Sweden, and that Swedes really know how to prepare fish better than anyone else. There are few places where fish is prepared so carefully and served so correctly.

Poached cod with grated horseradish, eggs, fresh shrimp and browned butter 4 SERVINGS

INGREDIENTS:

600 g (1 1/3 pounds) cod fillets, preferably cod loins
1 liter (4 cups) water
2 teaspoons salt
1 tablespoon canola oil
1 tablespoon butter

16 small new potatoes
1 liter (4 cups) water
1 tablespoon butter
2 dill stalks

TO SERVE:

4 eggs (*at room temperature*)
150 g (6 ounces) fresh shrimp *(in their shells)*
5 cm (2 inch length) fresh horseradish, grated
50 g (3 1/2 tablespoons) butter
2 dill stalks

DIRECTIONS:

1. Combine the water and salt, stirring until the salt is dissolved.

2. Cut the cod into four pieces of equal size, place in a deep dish and pour over the salt water to cover. Refrigerate for 3 hours.

3. Scrub and boil the new potatoes with butter and dill for 15–20 minutes depending upon their size.

4. Boil the eggs (heat water to boiling, add the eggs and let simmer for around 6 minutes), cool under cold water, peel and slice or cut into wedges.

5. Shell the shrimp.

6. Preheat the oven to 125 °C (250 °F).

7. Heat a frying pan. Add the oil, then the butter. When the butter has melted, add the cod. Fry the cod, skin side down (if still on), for 60 to 90 seconds, then turn and fry on the other side until nut brown, 30 to 60 seconds. Transfer to an ovenproof dish and place in the center of the oven for 6 to 10 minutes, depending upon the thickness. Optimal internal temperature for direct serving is 44–45 °C (111–113 °F).

8. While the fish is in the oven, brown the butter.

9. Place the potatoes in the middle of the plate. Arrange the egg slices/wedges and shrimp over the potatoes, then top with fish and grated horseradish. Pour over the browned butter. Garnish with dill strands.

Cod, eggs and shrimp are among my strongest childhood memories. When I was a child, we had a motorboat, and we spent every summer on the sea. Happiness was to catch some cod, then go to a nearby island, clean the fish and cook it over an open fire. Delicious!

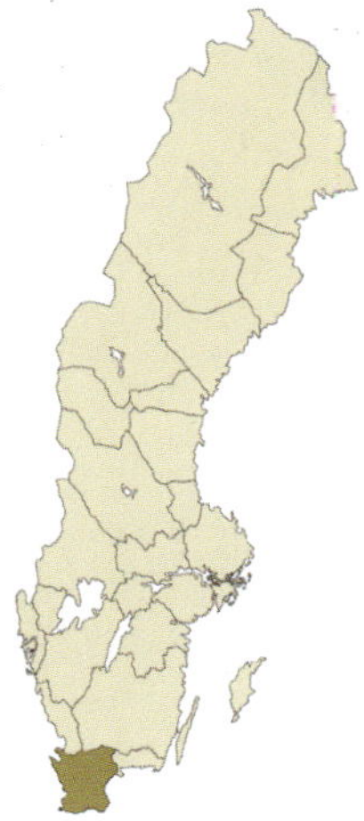

SKÅNE

Skåne is Sweden's premier culinary landscape. The average Scanian can be described as a lover of good food, often a jovial, slightly plump person who loves to say: "Good food, and lots of it, and at the right time!"

Skåne is Sweden's southernmost landscape, at the southernmost tip of the Scandinavian peninsula. It is densely populated (for Scandinavia), yet still dominated by agriculture. At the same time, the entire area is near the sea: The Baltic in the east, narrow Öresund that separates Sweden from Denmark and Copenhagen in the west, and farther north, the Kattegatt, which is part of the North Sea, takes over. It is close to Denmark, but also close to Germany and Poland.

Skåne has been Danish for much longer than it has been Swedish. It belonged to Denmark as early as Harald Bluetooth's time, during the latter part of the 10th century, and it did not become Swedish until the peace of Roskilde in 1658.

There are great plains in the south and west, with large scale agriculture on fertile fields, which are considered some of the best in the world. Skåne has the most cultivated soil in all of Sweden. Around 70 percent is dedicated to crops, fields or meadows. Grain, potatoes, sugar beets and rapeseed are grown here. The broad rolling fields of golden rapeseed flowers are just as photogenic as the cypress-clad hills of Tuscany.

But in Skåne, there are also forests, for the most part made up of deciduous trees, such as beech.

Österlen, along the southeastern coast, is a Swedish version of Provence, but with apples instead of grapes and olives. Many writers, musicians and artists live here, and there are lots of art galleries and lovely little restaurants.

The climate in Skåne is the warmest in Sweden, but it is also known for its white winters, when the snow falls over the open landscape like sand in a desert and creates large dunes.

Skåne is Sweden's answer to the southern states in the US: It has its own flag, and the dialect is full of diphthongs and at times difficult for other Swedes to understand.

LEFT: ALE'S STONES, KÅSEBERGA: A 67 METER (220 FEET) LONG MEGALITHIC STONE SHIP FORMED BY 59 LARGE SANDSTONE BOULDERS. ACCORDING TO FOLKLORE, LEGENDARY KING ALE IS BURIED HERE.
NEXT SPREAD: APPLE ART IN KIVIK, NEAR STENSHUVUD (ABOVE) BACKÅKRA (BELOW).

ABOVE: HILLS IN BRÖSARP.
NEXT SPREAD: A ROCKY BEACH NEAR KULLABERG.

Skåne is synonymous with good food. That's not unusual, since so much food is produced here. You can find the most and the best in Skåne. Some crops are grown on a large scale, but there is also a multitude of small-scale local production and artisanal foods.

Since the Middle Ages, there have been inns and guesthouses all over the landscape. Some are still in business, and many are worth a special journey.

And since Skåne has long been a wealthy area, there are also many venerable food traditions. Years ago, an eel feast was held in September; now the eel is endangered and has to be protected. September is also time for apples in Kivik in Österlen, and in November, St. Martin is feted with goose. And after that goose dinner, there's Skåne apple cake for dessert.

In the cuisine of Skåne, both traditions and seasons are important.

"Good food, and lots of it, and at the right time!"

Skåne apple cake 4 SERVINGS

INGREDIENTS:

2 dl (1 cup) water
1 dl (1/2 cup) sugar
8 medium sized tart apples
1 tablespoon potato starch
400 g (14 ounces) zwieback
100 g (4 ounces) white bread, preferably sourdough
3 tablespoons raw sugar
1 tablespoon cinnamon
100 g (3 1/2 ounces) butter

VANILLA SAUCE:

6 egg yolks
3 tablespoons sugar
3 dl (1 1/4 cups) cream
1 vanilla bean

DIRECTIONS:

1. Preheat the oven to 200 °C (400 °F).

2. Heat the sugar and water to boiling. Peel, core and cut 4 apples into small chunks. Cook in the sugar syrup for around 2 minutes. Transfer the apples with a slotted spoon to a blender and puree until smooth. Pour into a saucepan, stir the potato starch into a little cold water and stir into the apple puree. Heat to boiling, stirring constantly. Remove the pan from the heat as soon as the applesauce starts to bubble. Continue stirring for around 2 minutes.

3. Crush the zwieback and bread into crumbs (in a food processor) and fry in a dry pan over medium heat.

4. Sprinkle with sugar and cinnamon. Continue to fry until the crumbs turn golden brown. Add the butter and let it melt into the crumbs. Spread half the crumbs into a rectangular cake pan and press carefully.

5. Arrange half the apple puree over the crumbs.

6. Cut the remaining apples into narrow wedges (5 millimeters thick). Arrange half the apple wedges over the applesauce. Make another layer of crumbs, applesauce and apple wedges.

7. Bake in the middle of the oven for around 20 minutes.

8. Whisk the egg yolks, sugar and cream in a saucepan. Split the vanilla bean lengthwise and add. Heat until simmering, stirring constantly.

9. Whisk constantly. The heat should not be higher than 85°C (185°F), otherwise the eggs in the sauce will scramble. When you start to see steam rising, the temperature is about right. Whisk the sauce until it begins to thicken. Remove from the heat and place the pan into another pan of cold water to cool it down, whisking occasionally.

If you place a weight on the cake, it will become more compact and easier to cut into elegant slices. It is important to choose tart apples for this dish.

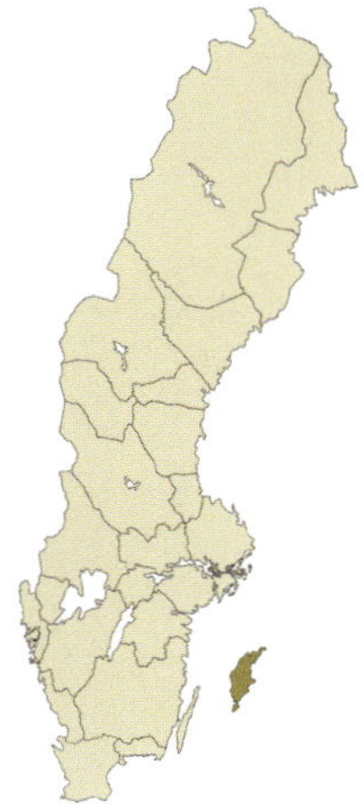

GOTLAND

Gotland is magical. It's like a separate little country out in the Baltic Sea, with a landscape that's different from everywhere else in Sweden, and with a long and interesting history. In the summer, it's as if the Mediterranean has moved up north.

Gotland is 90 kilometers east of the Swedish mainland. Its location, almost in the middle of the Baltic Sea, has made it an important center for both commerce and politics for centuries.

It was only natural that men from Gotland became sailors. Archaeological finds from the early Iron Age indicate that there were many contacts with foreign lands. During Viking times, Gotland became northern Europe's richest area, thanks to trade with far-off lands both to the east and to the west.

Visby became a commercial center, a place where the different nationalities met. Gotland's commercial and political role grew as the Hanseatic League became more powerful.

Today, the medieval center surrounded by the city wall is on the UNESCO World Heritage list.

There are reminders of Gotland's long and interesting history all over the island. There are 42,000 known ancient remains – almost 100 medieval churches, 400 large cairns from the Bronze Age and 1800 foundations and remains of buildings from the Iron Age.

The Gotland landscape is varied and magnificent, with meadows, wild cliffs, forests, cultivated fields and pastures. In the west, mighty cliffs rise from the sea. In the eastern lowlands, there are many kilometers of beaches – both of pebbles and of sand – that resemble those bordering the Mediterranean or even places farther south. Unusual limestone formations created by natural erosion, known as sea stacks, rise like petrified figures out of the sea. Gotland also boasts rich bird life and lush vegetation.

In the summer, thousands of tourists visit the island, and appropriately enough, Gotland is one of the places with the most sun in all of Sweden.

The small island of Fårö north of Gotland can be reached by ferry. Film director Ingmar Bergman lived here. Around Fårö, there are many stretches of sea stacks.

LEFT: VISBY CITY WALL.
NEXT SPREAD: A STREET, ROMA ABBEY, SEA STACKS BY THE OLD HARBOR, FÅRÖ, A STONE WALL, FÅRÖ.

PREVIOUS SPREAD: VISBY CITY WALL IN THE EARLY MORNING MIST.

THE BEACH AT SNÄCK, KOVIK'S FISHING VILLAGE (PAGE 32). LANGHAMMARS, FÅRÖ (ABOVE). SYSSNE POINT (AT LEFT).

Gotland is an active food island, with many farmers, artisanal producers, specialty food shops, farm shops, restaurants and cafés.

The earliest carrots and asparagus are found here. And there are truffles. Sheep and cattle graze on meadows that border the sea. Local grain is stone ground into flour, and small farm dairies make cheeses from sheep, goat and cow milk.

Beer is also brewed on the island, including the local drink, *Gotlandsdricke*, a strong smoky ale flavored with juniper, hops and malt. The mild climate even allows wine to be produced here, and different spirits are made with local raw materials.

And the sea yields its own treasures, such as salmon, herring, turbot and flounder.

Saffron oven pancake is a Gotland specialty. We don't know how saffron got to Gotland, but maybe it was the result of all the foreign commerce. Now, there is small scale production of the saffron crocus on the island.

Traditionally, saffron oven pancake is served with blue raspberry jam. These are related to blackberries and taste rather like raspberries, but they are a matte blue color. Blue raspberries grow in lime-rich soil in southern Sweden and ripen in late summer.

Saffron oven pancake

4 SERVINGS

INGREDIENTS:

- 1 1/2 dl (2/3 cup) short grain rice
- 3 dl (1 1/4 cups) water
- 1/2 teaspoon salt
- 1 tablespoon sugar
- 1 1/2 tablespoons butter
- 3 dl (1 1/4 cups) cream
- 4 dl (1 2/3 cups) milk
- 50 g (2/3 cup) thinly sliced almonds
- 1 packet (1/2 gram/large pinch) saffron
- 2 tablespoons sugar
- 2 dl (3/4 cup) whipping cream
- 3 eggs

DIRECTIONS:

1. Add the rice to the water and cook with the salt, sugar and butter for around 20 minutes. Add the cream and milk and let simmer for 20 more minutes.
2. Remove the pan from the heat and let the rice cool, stirring often.
3. Preheat the oven to 225 °C (425 °F). Sprinkle the almonds on a dry baking sheet. Toast, stirring every other minute, until they turn nut brown. This should take 4–8 minutes.
4. Reduce the oven temperature to 200 °C (400 °F).
5. Crush the saffron with the sugar in a mortar.
6. Whip the cream.
7. In another bowl, beat the eggs and saffron-sugar until thick and lemon-colored, fold in the whipped cream, then the almonds and finally the rice porridge.
8. Pour into a greased ovenproof dish. Bake in the center of the oven for around 25 minutes.

A saffron oven pancake is not supposed to be too sweet or too heavy. It is best when light and fluffy and is served lukewarm with lightly whipped cream and raspberry jam. On Gotland, saffron oven pancake is served with blue raspberry jam, but it can be difficult to find off the island.

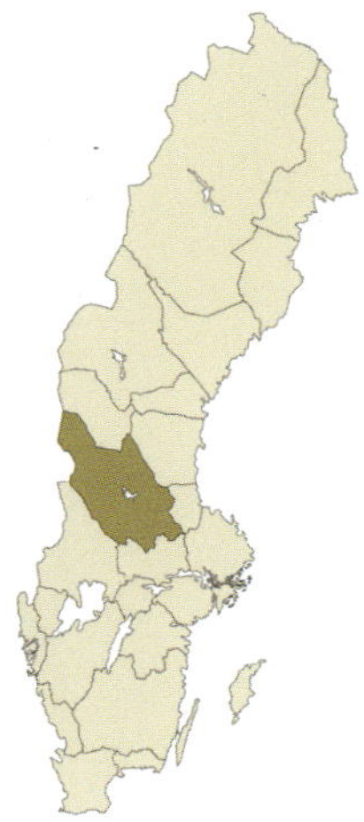

DALARNA

Many, including most Swedes, think of Dalarna as Sweden in miniature. It is here, on bright green blossoming meadows alongside a clear lake, that midsummer is celebrated with dance and song.

Dalarna is in central Sweden, in northwest Svealand, only a few hours from Stockholm. Although it is most often associated with lively summer days, Dalarna also has a typical Swedish winter, with the most snow in southern Sweden.

Mother Nature has graced Dalarna with mountains in the northwest and plains in the southeast. Lakes and rivers add character, with Lake Siljan in the center, and the Västerdal and Österdal rivers meet to form the mighty Dala river. Lake Siljan was formed by a meteorite that crashed to earth around 260 million years ago and gave it its circular shape.

Mining in the south has been a major industry for centuries. Copper was already being produced during the ninth and tenth centuries. The Falun copper mine was Sweden's main source of income for hundreds of years. Now the mine is on the UNESCO World Heritage list.

The people of Dalarna have played important roles in Swedish politics for centuries, and they are characterized by their strong will and love of independence.

Dalarna as Sweden in miniature was an image created around 1900, during the national romantic period, when the concept of a Swedish identity was very important. Some of the costumes, dances and folk music which are considered typically Swedish were created during that time.

Artist Carl Larsson was originally from Stockholm, but he made Dalarna his home, and he painted watercolors of idyllic family life from his farm, Sundborn. Artist Anders Zorn was born in Dalarna, as was poet Dan Andersson and opera singer Jussi Björling.

Every year folk music enthusiasts and fiddlers get together for big festivals. And traditional painting can still be seen on decorative wooden Dala horses of all sizes.

Dalarna is also known for the oldest and longest cross-country ski race – Vasaloppet – always held on the first Sunday in March. This is a 90 km (56 mile) long ski marathon with 10,000 skiers. Its summer counterpart is the Vansbro open water swimming competition, one of the world's largest, the second week in July.

LEFT: STABLES NEAR RÄTTVIK CHURCH.
NEXT SPREAD: RAISING THE MAYPOLE IN RÄTTVIK.

LEFT: LAKE SILJAN, A FOLK MUSICIAN. **ABOVE:** SILJANSNÄS NATURE RESERVE.
NEXT SPFEAD: MUSICIAN JOHN ERIK EGGENS, A CHURCH-BOAT, SILJAN, FOREST OUTSIDE RÄTTVIK.

Crispbread is the most Swedish of all breads. No Swede moves abroad without solving the problem of how to find crispbread. Traditionally, it is baked with rye flour. It is either rolled out into thin, flat sheets, as in this recipe, or a special crispbread rolling pin with pegs on it is used to roll out sheets with characteristic holes.

Crispbread rounds were made with a hole in the middle so that they could be threaded onto a pole and hung under the roof. They can be stored almost indefinitely due to their very low water content.

Dalarna and the bordering area of Värmland are the heart of the crispbread belt. Leksand and Falun have given their names to special types of crispbread, and in Dala-Järna, at the Pyramid bakery, the Egyptian flat bread tradition meets the Swedish.

Thin crispbread 4 SERVINGS

INGREDIENTS:

2 dl (1 cup) milk
50 g (1 3/4 ounces) fresh yeast
4 dl (2 cups) coarse rye flour
1 1/2 tablespoons caraway seed
1 tablespoon salt flakes
4 dl (2 cups) all-purpose flour

DIRECTIONS:

1. Heat the milk to body temperature (37–40 °C/98–102 °F). Add the yeast, stirring until dissolved. Mix in the rye flour, caraway seed, salt and almost half of the all-purpose flour. Knead to form a stiff dough, beginning with a wooden spoon, continuing by hand. Knead in the rest of the flour until the dough is smooth and not sticky. Sprinkle with a little flour and let rise for 30–40 minutes. A pasta machine is useful for rolling thin sheets of dough. Otherwise, sprinkle the work surface with flour first, then place the dough on it and sprinkle the dough with more flour. Roll to a thickness of 1–2 millimeters.

2. Preheat the oven to 225 °C (425 °F).

3. Cut the dough into the desired shape – square, round or even free-form. Bake for 6–8 minutes, turn off the oven and open the door. Remove the crispbread when it is completely dry. Store in a dry and airy place.

This is a basic recipe that can be varied with different flavorings. Try seasoning it with thyme, rosemary, lemon zest or fennel.

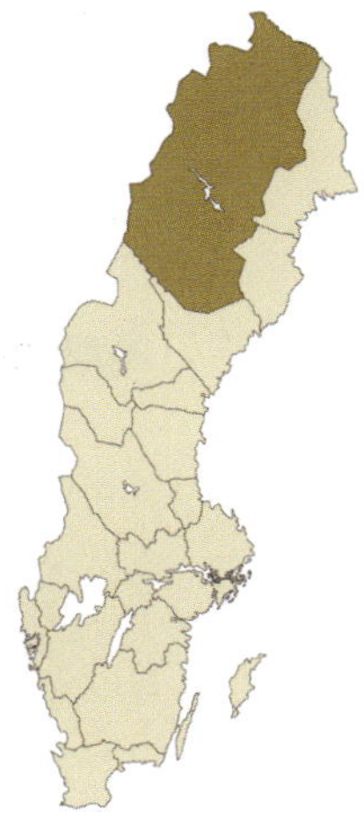

LAPPLAND 

Lappland is often called Europe's last wilderness. With magical and unique natural phenomena, such as Lapporten, near the top of the northwestern part of the region, a two-kilometer (1 1/4 mile) wide u-shaped valley between the mountain peaks Tjuonatjåkko and Nissuntjårro.

Mighty Lappland is Sweden's largest region and makes up more than one fourth of the country's geographical area. To give a better idea, it's larger than Portugal. However, only 100 000 people, just over 1 percent of Sweden's population, live here. That translates to less than one person per square kilometer.

Lappland is primarily Mother Nature's domain. In the west are mountains devoid of vegetation, with Kebnekaise, Sweden's highest peak, at 3111 meters (6926 feet). Sweden boasts of twelve peaks over 2000 meters (6562 feet), and all are in Lappland.

There are also forests of low mountain birch and tundra, where only low bushes and grass can grow in the eternally frozen soil. Many flowers grow on the lower parts of the slopes.

Temperatures can sink to shivering −40 °C (−40 °F), but the average temperature in January is between −10 and −15 °C (14 and 5 °F).

Farther east are evergreen forests and marshes where the beloved cloudberry grows.

Rushing rivers and thousands of lakes offer a variety of fish, including char, trout, grayling, whitefish and salmon.

Both the red fox and the arctic fox are native to Lappland, and the region is also home to wolverine, lynx and brown bear. And there is a rich bird life.

Lappland was populated by the Sami, who were nomads, until the early 1600s, when mines were established in the region and Swedes moved in. Sápmi is the Sami name for Sameland or Lappland, which extends beyond Sweden's borders to include parts of Norway, Finland and the Kola peninsula in Russia. There are around 20 000 Sami in Sweden and 80 000 in all of Sápmi. Around ten percent of Swedish Sami work with reindeer.

There are nine national parks and many trails in Lappland. If you visit in the summer, you can experience the Midnight Sun, when the sun never completely disappears below the horizon.

LEFT: LAPPORTEN.
NEXT SPREAD: TORNETRÄSK (ABOVE), VIEW FROM BJÖRKLIDEN (BELOW).

Kratersjön 2,5
0,5 Björkliden

ABOVE: THE FALLS AT BJÖRKLIDEN.
NEXT SPREAD: LAPPORTEN AT DUSK.

Traditional Sami food is dominated by reindeer meat and fish. Thinly shaved reindeer meat that can be sautéed quickly is a product found in the frozen food department of most Swedish supermarkets, even far down south. *Souvas* is salted and cold-smoked reindeer meat that is cut into strips and fried in butter. This dish has been praised by the Slow Food movement.

Cloudberries grow in the marshes of Lappland. They tolerate the cold very well and survive temperatures down to –40 °C (–40 °F). All Swedes love cloudberries, and they grow as far south as Skåne. But they are associated mostly with the north and are loved and used the most there. In good years, hundreds of tons of these orange berries can be harvested. A lot are frozen or made into jam and even liqueur.

Cloudberry parfait is the perfect ending to a Lappland menu with reindeer or other game or fish.

Cloudberry parfait 4 SERVINGS

INGREDIENTS:

3 eggs
1 dl (scant 1/2 cup) sugar
3 dl (1 1/4 cups) whipping cream
3 dl (1 1/4 cups) cloudberries

DIRECTIONS:

1. Whisk the eggs and sugar in a metal mixing bowl over a simmering water bath until thickened. Let cool.
2. Whip the cream and fold into the egg mixture.
3. Carefully stir in the berries and pour into a rinsed mold. Freeze overnight or for at least 4 to 5 hours.

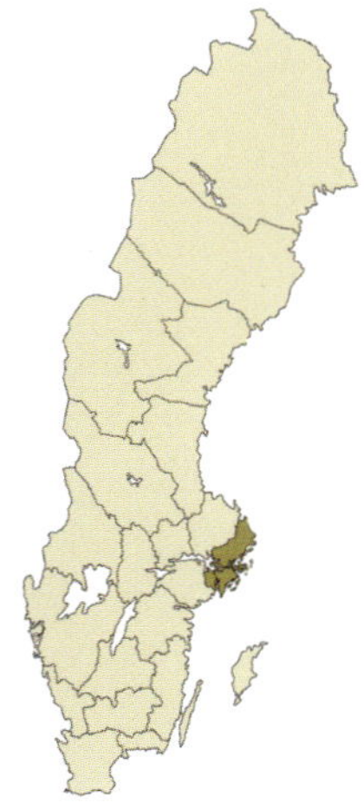

STOCKHOLM

Welcome to one of the most beautiful capital cities in the world. Stockholm is often called the "Venice of the North" for good reason, as the city is built on islands.

Stockholm is located where fresh water meets seawater, where the great Lake Mälaren meets the Baltic Sea. A natural place to build a city during a time when the most effective means of getting around was on the water.

Eventually Stockholm became the largest and most important center of commerce for trade with the countries bordering the Baltic Sea and Germany, and it was also a natural seat of power.

The name Stockholm first appeared in print during the 13th century. "Stock" probably derives from the piles that were driven into the bottom of the sound to serve as a defense between Lakes Mälaren and Salt. "Holm" probably comes from Stadsholmen, the island where the Old Town is today.

During the 17th century, Sweden became a great power in Europe, and the population of the city grew six-fold in a short time.

What was earlier a Viking seafaring and industrial city is now dominated by the service and governmental sectors with 85 percent of all employment.

Stockholm is Sweden's main tourist destination. The city center is built over 14 islands that are connected with 57 bridges. A third of the city's area is made up of water, so it isn't at all wrong to compare it with Venice. Stockholm's city hall adds to that, inspired as it was by the Campanile and Doge's Palace on St. Mark's Square in Venice. Swedish author and Nobel prizewinner Selma Lagerlöf writes that Stockholm is a city that swims on the water. The city is also called the queen of Lake Mälaren.

Stockholm is Sweden's largest city with just over two million inhabitants in the greater city area, but it is a small city on the world scale. Even though it has been settled for over 1000 years, there is still untouched nature just a few kilometers from the center of town. Forty percent of greater Stockholm is composed of parks and green areas, and there are eight nature reserves.

Who would believe that Stockholm is located at the same latitude as the southern tip of Greenland?

LEFT: KULTURHUSET (CULTURAL CENTER) WITH KLARA CHURCH
NEXT SPREAD: A MEDICI LION ON THE SLOPE UP TO STOCKHOLM PALACE

LEFT: VIEW OF THE CITY HALL TOWER, A STREET IN THE OLD TOWN, VIEW OF THE CITY HALL FROM THE LION SLOPE AND BATHING IN LAKE MÄLAREN. **ABOVE:** RIDDARHOLM CHURCH.
NEXT SPREAD: HUVUDSKÄR IN STOCKHOLM'S ARCHIPELAGO.

Outside the Slussen subway station on the island of Södermalm is a cart that could sell hot dogs, but according to the yellow sign in the shape of a fish on its roof, fried Baltic herring is served here.

This classic is simply fried Baltic herring on crispbread, just as in the recipe below. A heartier version serves it with potato puree and lingonberry jam. And a more modern version is the herring-burger. Simple, luxurious and typically Swedish, and very Stockholm.

Baltic herring is old-fashioned Swedish food, the food of the poor. Herring was always plentiful, and it was cheap. And it still is.

Baltic herring and regular herring are the same species, but they swim in different waters. If caught north of Kristianopel in northeastern Blekinge, it is called Baltic herring. It is often shorter and leaner than regular herring. The lower the salt content of the water, the shorter the fish.

Fried Baltic herring with dill butter and pickled red onions

4–6 OPEN-FACE SANDWICHES

INGREDIENTS:

400 g (14 ounces) Baltic herring fillets
1 tablespoon salt
1/4 teaspoon ground allspice
1/4 teaspoon freshly ground white pepper
3 dill stalks
1 tablespoon cold-pressed canola oil
1/2 dl (3 1/2 tablespoons) mild sweet mustard
2 dl (1 cup) rye flour
50 g (3 1/2 tablespoons) butter

DILL BUTTER:

50 g (3 1/2 tablespoons) butter, softened
1 tablespoon cold-pressed canola oil
3–4 dill stalks

DIRECTIONS:

1. Rinse the herring well in a colander under running cold water. Season with salt, allspice and pepper.
2. Remove the thick stalks and mix the dill strands with the oil and mustard. Spread the inside of the fillets with the mustard mixture. Sandwich two fillets together, skin side out and dredge in rye flour.
3. Melt the butter in a hot pan and let it turn golden brown. Add the fish and fry over medium heat for around 2 minutes per side, until cooked through.
4. Dill butter: Remove the thick stalks and place the dill strands in a blender with the oil and blend until it turns green. Add the butter and blend until the dill is thoroughly mixed into the butter.
5. Spread dill butter on crisp-bread, top with fried herring and pickled red onions.

Pickled red onions

CA 500 ML (2 CUPS) JAR

INGREDIENTS:

5 red onions
1/4 lemon
2 1/4 dl (1 cup) water
3/4 dl (1/3 cup) 12% vinegar
1 1/2 dl (2/3 cup) sugar

DIRECTIONS:

1. Peel and thinly slice the onions. Cut 2–3 slices of lemon.
2. Combine the water, vinegar and sugar in a saucepan and heat to boiling, stirring to dissolve the sugar. Let simmer for around 2 minutes.
3. Add the red onions, reheat to boiling and let simmer for around 30 seconds. Add the lemon and simmer for 30 seconds more. Pour into a glass jar, seal and store in the refrigerator.

BELOVED CLASSICS

Sweden is much more than the culinary and geographical stops so far in this book. On the following pages, we will present even more beloved classics. Dishes and baked goods that are typically Swedish but are not connected with any particular region. And they are delicious wherever they are made and eaten.

Herring is often on the menu for festive occasions. Herring at midsummer. Herring at Christmas. Herring at Easter. The former poor man's food has become festive, yet it is still inexpensive to buy.

In earlier times, pickling was a means of preservation. The brine made from vinegar, sugar and water kept the herring from spoiling so fast. The classic brine is called 1-2-3 brine because it is composed of one part 12 % vinegar, two parts sugar and three parts water.

The easiest and most popular pickled herring, which is called just that, includes onions, carrots, allspice and black pepper. Other classic flavors are onion herring, French onion herring (made with French vinegar) and creamy mustard herring. There are many ways to pickle herring and every year, there are new flavor combinations.

Herring isn't just delicious, it is also healthy, with its high concentration of omega-3 fatty acids.

Pickled herring AROUND 6 SERVINGS

INGREDIENTS:

1/2 red onion
2 dl (1 scant cup) 12 % vinegar
4 1/2 dl (1 3/4 cups) water
3 dl (1 1/4 cups) sugar
12 whole allspice berries
6 bay leaves
8 white peppercorns
1 teaspoon caraway seed
4 star anise
300 g (10 1/2 ounces) pre-soaked herring fillets

DIRECTIONS:

1. Peel and cut the red onions into narrow strips.
2. Combine the vinegar, water and sugar in a saucepan and stir until the sugar dissolves. Heat to boiling and let simmer for around 5 minutes.
3. Toast the spices in a dry hot frying pan for around one minute. Add to the vinegar mixture and let simmer for around 2 minutes. Add the onion and then remove the saucepan from the heat.
4. Let the brine cool.
5. Rinse the herring carefully and cut into thin slices (around 1 cm or 3/8 inch). Layer in a glass jar alternately with the spiced brine.
6. The herring can be served immediately, but it will taste better if the flavors are allowed to develop for 2 to 3 days in the refrigerator.

There are endless ways to flavor vinegar brine. Add berries such as black currents, lingonberries, cherries, sea buckthorn and rosehip. Even lemon, line and orange zest, as well as fresh herbs such as dill, oregano, basil and thyme can be used to flavor herring.

In Scandinavia, marinated salmon dates back at least to the 14th century. In the olden days, when too much salmon was caught, the fish was lightly salted and buried in the ground. The result was a sour fermented salmon more like the famous or infamous Swedish dish sour Baltic herring. Today, the salmon is marinated with sugar and salt, and the cells of the fish are broken down by the fish's own enzymes.

Marinated salmon with coffee-mustard sauce 4 SERVINGS

This recipe must be prepared 48 hours before serving.

INGREDIENTS:

400 g (14 ounces) salmon loin fillet
3 tablespoons sugar
2 tablespoons salt
2 teaspoons aquavit, preferably Gammel Norrlands
3 dill stalks

DIRECTIONS:

1. Use fresh-frozen salmon that is defrosted just before needed.

2. Clean your hands and kitchen tools thoroughly.

3. Remove any dark areas that are found between the fish and the skin. Be sure to remove all bones.

4. Combine the sugar and salt and sprinkle it onto a dish. Roll the fish in the mixture, so that it is completely covered with sugar-salt. Transfer the salmon to a plastic bag, seal and refrigerate for 24 hours.

5. Day 2: Rub with aquavit and wrap or coat the fish with dill. Return it to the plastic bag and refrigerate for 24 hours more. Then the fish is ready to serve.

6. Remove the dill, cut the salmon into even slices and garnish with new, fresh dill.

Coffee-mustard sauce is probably my best and most popular cold sauce. It is best with marinated salmon but it is also good with meat dishes.

Coffee-mustard sauce 8–12 SERVINGS

INGREDIENTS:

1 dl (scant 1/2 cup) Swedish medium-strong mustard
1 dl (scant 1/2 cup) raw sugar
3/4 dl (1/3 cup) white wine vinegar
2 tablespoons honey
2 dl (scant 1 cup) cold-pressed canola oil
Salt
1 tablespoon brown sugar
1/2 dl (3 1/2 tablespoons) strong coffee (or 1 double espresso)

DIRECTIONS:

1. Combine the mustard, raw sugar, vinegar and honey in a bowl.

2. Whisk until the sugar is completely dissolved. Important! Add the canola oil in a thin stream, whisking constantly.

3. Season with salt, brown sugar and coffee (or espresso).

Skagen mixture gets its name from Toast Skagen, a dish that did not originate in Denmark, in spite of its name. It was invented during the 1950s by legendary restaurateur Tore Wretman.

Old man's mix (herring-egg salad) makes Swedes think of summer inns and local hotels with white tablecloths, where people enjoyed a lunch of herring, cheese and butter chased by flavored spirits (*snaps*). Most people who ordered this lunch were men, which is also true of the herring-egg salad known as "old man's mix".

Souvas means smoked in the Sami language and is cold-smoked reindeer meat. In earlier times, lightly salted meat was hung up by the smoke hole in the tent where the Sami lived. Now there are special tents for smoking.

Three mixtures: Skagen, Old man's mix and Reindeer mix with souvas

4–6 SERVINGS

Skagen mix

INGREDIENTS:

400 g (14 ounces) fresh shrimp in their shells (around 200 g/7 ounces without shells)
1 cm (1/2 inch) fresh horseradish
1/2 dl (3 1/2 tablespoons) chopped dill
3/4 dl (1/3 cup) mayonnaise
1/4 dl (2 tablespoons) crème fraiche or sour cream
Salt and pepper
2 teaspoons Dijon mustard

DIRECTIONS:

1. Shell and coarsely chop the shrimp.
2. Grate the horseradish, chop the dill and combine with the mayonnaise, crème fraiche and shrimp.
3. Season with salt, pepper and Dijon mustard.

Gubbhyllan Restaurant's old man's mix

INGREDIENTS:

3 eggs
3 small potatoes
3 matjes herring fillets
1 tart apple
1 small red onion
1/2 dl (3 1/2 tablespoons) finely chopped chives
1/2 dl (3 1/2 tablespoons) finely chopped dill

DIRECTIONS:

1. Hardcook the egg (around 8 minutes) and boil the potatoes. Refrigerate.
2. Chop all ingredients into fine dice and combine.

There are many classic variations of this mix, and many use anchovies instead of matjes herring. For some, apples and potatoes are not traditional ingredients, but I think they work beautifully and that the tart apple adds the perfect touch.

Reindeer mix with suovas

INGREDIENTS:

200 g (7 ounces) suovas (smoked reindeer)
1 dl (scant 1/2 cup) parsley
1 red onion
3/4 dl (1/3 cup) mayonnaise
1/4 dl (2 tablespoons) crème fraiche or sour cream
1 tablespoon whole grain mustard
Salt and pepper

DIRECTIONS:

1. Cut the smoked reindeer into fine dice, chop the onion and parsley, and combine with the mayonnaise and crème fraiche. Season to taste with mustard, salt and pepper.

Suovas, which means smoked in the Sami language, is salted and smoked reindeer meat. Suovas is one of the oldest means of food preservation in Sweden. The meat is salted for a few days before it is smoked.

Traditionally, and still at lunch restaurants and school cafeterias, this dish is served on Thursdays. The dish and its connection with Thursdays goes back to the Middle Ages. Thursdays were meat days, and Fridays were meatless days, which means that most people ate fish, according to the Catholic fasting rules. Now the soup is often followed by pancakes with jam for dessert. On special occasions, warm Swedish arrack *punsch* is served alongside.

Gubbhyllan Restaurant's pea soup with fried salt pork 4 SERVINGS

INGREDIENTS:

5 dl (2 cups) dried yellow peas
1 1/2 liters (6 1/3 cups) water
Salt
1/2 liter (2 cups) vegetable stock
10 black peppercorns
4 thyme branches
2 teaspoons dried thyme
2 teaspoons dried marjoram
1 onion
1 carrot
Pepper
4 tablespoons mustard, preferably Skåne-style
200 g (7 ounces) salt pork

DIRECTIONS:

DAY 1

1. Soak the peas in a generous amount of water. Drain and refill with water at least once. Let sit overnight. Drain.

DAY 2

2. Boil the peas in a large pot with the salted water and stock. Add the peppercorns, thyme and marjoram. Slice the onion and quarter the carrot lengthwise and add. Let the soup simmer for around 2 hours, stirring every 10 minutes or so.
3. Skim off any scum and hulls that float to the surface.
4. Add water if the soup gets too thick.
5. Season with salt, pepper and half the mustard.
6. Cut the pork into 1 cm (3/8 inch) cubes. Fry in a hot pan with no added fat. Divide the pork among four soup bowls and pour over the soup. Garnish with mustard.

Traditionally, the pork was cooked with the soup, but I think it tastes better when it is fried separately.

This soup is also delicious when served with cold Swedish arrack punsch.

Not many years ago, salmon was considered a luxury, but these days, farmed salmon has once again become everyday food. In the olden days, salmon was so plentiful that workers had it written into their contracts that they were not to eat salmon too many days per week. In those days, all salmon was wild, not farmed.

Salmon pudding with melted butter and green peas 4 SERVINGS

INGREDIENTS:

800 g (1 3/4 pounds) potatoes, preferably firm and waxy
1 bunch dill
2 onions
Butter *(for frying and greasing the pan)*
600 g (1 1/3 pounds) salmon fillets
4 eggs
2 dl (1 cup) cream
2 dl (1 cup) milk
Salt and pepper
400 g (14 ounces) green peas
50 g (3 1/2 tablespoons) butter

DIRECTIONS:

1. Peel and boil the potatoes with some of the dill. Drain and let the potatoes cool.

2. Preheat the oven to 200 °C (400 °F).

3. Peel and thinly slice the onions. Fry in butter until golden brown.

4. Slice the salmon and chop the remaining dill.

5. Whisk together the eggs, cream and milk and season with salt and pepper. The mixture should be quite salty because it will flavor both the potatoes and the salmon.

6. Grease an ovenproof dish with butter.

7. Slice the potatoes and layer potatoes, salmon, onion and dill (but save a little dill for garnish) in two or three layers.

8. Pour the egg mixture evenly over the layers and bake for 35 to 40 minutes, depending upon the thickness of the pudding.

9. Heat the water to boiling and add the peas. Cook for around 15 seconds, then drain. Sprinkle with salt.

10. Melt the butter in a saucepan and skim off the white protein that bubbles up. When the butter is pale golden brown, it is ready to serve.

11. Garnish the pudding with the remaining dill and the peas. Drizzle melted butter over and serve immediately.

This dish has its roots in the traditional farming culture, which is not all that far back in time. It was not until after World War II that Swedes left the countryside and moved to the city. Sweet-and-sour side dishes, such as lingonberries with meatballs and apples with pork, are popular in Swedish country cooking.

Pork belly with apples 4–6 SERVINGS

INGREDIENTS:

1 kg (2 1/2 pounds) boneless pork belly without rind
20 g (1 tablespoon) salt
30 g (2 1/2 tablespoons) sugar
1 onion
4 thyme branches
1/2 lemon

2 apples
2 flat-leaf parsley stalks
Pickled onions *(see recipe page 64)*

DIRECTIONS:

DAY 1

1. Combine the salt and sugar and rub the mixture into the meat. Place in a plastic bag and refrigerate overnight.

DAY 2

2. Remove the meat from the refrigerator one hour before cooking. If there are remnants of sugar and salt on the meat, rinse quickly under cold water and dry well with paper towels.

3. Preheat the oven to 250 °C (450 °F). Lower the speed of the oven fan, if possible. Place the meat on a rack, fat side up.

4. Peel and slice the onion and place on the meat. Sprinkle the meat with thyme. Cut the lemon into thin slices and place on top of the thyme and onions.

5. Place the meat in the middle of the oven with a pan underneath to catch the melted fat that drips off.

6. Bake for 60 minutes. Baste with the fat every 6 minutes. Lower the oven temperature to 150 °C (300 °F) and bake for 2 more hours, basting every 12 minutes. That is a total of 3 hours cooking time.

7. Rinse the apples. Core them and cut each into 8 wedges.

8. Place the apple wedges on a parchment-covered baking sheet. Drizzle with 2 tablespoons fat from the pan. Thirty minutes before the meat is finished roasting, place the baking sheet with the apples over the meat. Bake for 20–25 minutes.

9. Remove the parsley leaves from the stalks and cut into shreds. Stir into the pickled onions.

10. Remove the apples from the oven when they begin to wrinkle. Combine with the parsley and pickled onions.

11. Just before serving, baste the meat one more time. Scrape off the onions, thyme and lemon and cut into slices. Serve with the apple salad or with potato puree or boiled potatoes and a green salad.

I vary this dish according to the season. At Christmas, I like to season it with cloves, rosemary or thin slices of fresh ginger.

You can also use orange or lime instead of lemon to add citrus flavor.

Meatballs are probably the most beloved dish in all of Swedish country cooking. Enjoyed by children of all ages! And of course, homemade meatballs are always best, and there are many different recipes. Lingonberry compote and cream sauce complete the meal. IKEA has introduced the Swedish meatball to the rest of the world.

Meatballs with potato puree, lingonberry compote and pickled cucumbers

35–40 MEATBALLS

INGREDIENTS:

2 potatoes, preferably mealy, such as King Edward
1 dl (1/2 cup) cream
2 1/2 tablespoons game or mushroom stock
1 dl (1/2 cup) breadcrumbs
2 onions
Butter
Salt and pepper
200 g (7 ounces) ground reindeer or deer or beef
300 g (10 1/2 ounces) ground beef
400 g (14 ounces) ground pork
1 egg
1/2 dl (3 1/2 tablespoons) water
1 teaspoon brown sugar
2 tablespoons dried chanterelles *(or other dried mushrooms)*, crushed into powder

POTATO PUREE:

1 kg (2 1/4 pounds) potatoes, preferably mealy
1 dl (1/3 cup) cream
2 dl (2/3 cup) milk
2 tablespoons butter
Salt and pepper
Grated nutmeg

LINGONBERRY COMPOTE:

200 g (7 ounces) lingonberries (frozen)
100 g (1/2 cup) sugar

PICKLED CUCUMBERS:

3/4 dl (1/3 cup) 12% vinegar
1/2 dl (2/3 cup) sugar
3 dl (1 1/4 cups) water
1 teaspoon yellow mustard seed
10 black peppercorns
1 large snake cucumber
3–4 dill crowns

DIRECTIONS:

1. Preheat the oven to 150°C (300°F).

2. Boil the potatoes in their skins, peel and press through a ricer.

3. Combine the cream, stock and breadcrumbs.

4. Peel and mince the onion. Brown in 1 tablespoon butter in a hot pan.

5. Combine all the ingredients and season with salt and pepper. Make a small meatball and fry it to see if the seasonings are correct. Make meatballs of desired size and brown them all over in butter. Transfer to an ovenproof dish and bake for 8–10 minutes.

6. Peel and boil the potatoes. Combine the cream, milk and butter in a saucepan and heat.

7. Press the potatoes, add the cream mixture and mix to a smooth, airy puree. Season with salt, pepper and nutmeg.

8. Place the frozen cleaned lingonberries in a bowl and pour over the sugar. Let the sugar defrost the berries and mingle with their own juices. It's a good idea to start the process at least 5 hours before serving. It is possible to mix immediately, but the berries won't be so firm.

9. Combine the vinegar, sugar, water, mustard and pepper in a saucepan and heat to boiling, stirring occasionally. Rinse the cucumber and cut into thin slices. Place the cucumber slices in a glass jar, add the dill crowns and fill with vinegar brine.

Clean the chanterelles and dry them carefully over a long time. When they are completely dried, place in a blender and run at high speed until they become powder. Use as a seasoning in ground meat mixtures, sauces and casseroles. In Sweden, chanterelle season lasts from August to October.

Cabbage rolls are related to the Turkish *dolmasi*, but they did not come back with Swedish soldiers who had been in Turkey. It is thought that they were introduced by Turks who settled in Stockholm in the beginning of the 18th century to demand repayment of money lent to the Swedish king Karl XII.

Cabbage rolls 4 SERVINGS

INGREDIENTS:

2 1/2 dl (1 cup) cream
1 dl (1/3 cup) milk
3/4 dl (1/3 cup) breadcrumbs
1 cabbage
Salt
1 onion
75 g (2 1/2 ounces) butter
2 boiled potatoes
500 g (1 1/4 pounds) ground beef and pork
2 eggs
1 tablespoon light sugar syrup or corn syrup
3 tablespoons beef stock
1 tablespoon brown sugar
Salt and pepper

DIRECTIONS:

1. Combine the cream, milk and breadcrumbs.

2. Remove the central core of the cabbage. Heat salted water (1/2 tablespoon salt per liter/quart water) to boiling, add the cabbage. Make sure that the water covers the cabbage completely. Let simmer for around 20 minutes.

3. Remove the cabbage from the water and loosen the leaves. Remove the thick middle stalk.

4. Preheat the oven to 200 °C (400 °F).

5. Peel and chop the onion and remaining small bits of cabbage. Brown in butter in a frying pan. Mash the potatoes and add to the onion mixture. Place the meat in a bowl, add the onion mixture and the cream-breadcrumb mixture, along with the syrup, stock and brown sugar. Mix thoroughly and season with salt and pepper.

6. Arrange individual cabbage leaves on a board. Place a spoonful of meat mixture in the center of each, fold the sides over the meat and then roll up.

7. Place seam side down in an ovenproof dish and bake in the center of the oven for around 25 minutes.

8. Serve with boiled potatoes and natural juices flavored with red wine.

Swedish country cooking often utilizes cheap front quarter beef, such as chuck. In the Skåne version of this beef stew, the meat is cut into cubes, while in the rest of Sweden, it is made with pounded slices.

Beef stew with pickled beets 4–6 SERVINGS

INGREDIENTS:

1 1/2 kg (3 1/3 pounds) beef chuck or stew meat
1 onion
2 carrots
Butter *(for frying)*
2 teaspoons all-purpose flour
8 bay leaves
12 allspice berries
5 cloves
2 dl (1 cup) red wine
4 dl (1 2/3 cups) beef stock
4 dl (1 2/3 cups) water
Salt and pepper

DIRECTIONS:

1. Cut the meat into 3–4 cm (1 1/2 inch) chunks.
2. Peel and cut the onion and carrots into chunks.
3. Brown the meat thoroughly in the butter.
4. Sprinkle with flour and stir to coat.
5. Add the vegetables and spices and pour over the liquids.
6. Cover and let simmer for around 2 hours, adding more water if it dries out.

Pickled beets 8–12 SERVINGS

INGREDIENTS:

500 g (1 1/4 pounds) beets
1 dl (1/3 cup) 12 % vinegar
2 dl (2/3 cup) sugar
3 dl (1 cup) water
5 allspice berries

DIRECTIONS:

1. Scrub and rinse the beets. Let simmer for 25–35 minutes, depending upon their size.
2. Combine the remaining ingredients and heat to boiling.
3. Peel the beets and cut into slices or wedges as desired. Place in a glass jar and cover with the brine.

In the past, the best meal of the week was on Sunday, and in many places, that is still true today. And it was served in the dining room. Otherwise, that room was reserved for birthdays, christenings and funerals. Meat was always on the menu, a big joint roasted in the oven, and most often roasted for too long, so that it turned grey and dry. But then there was always enough gravy to disguise that!

Roast moose with gravy, root vegetables and pickled chanterelles

4 SERVINGS

INGREDIENTS:

800 g (1 3/4 pounds) boneless moose *(or beef)* roast
2 tablespoons sugar
1 tablespoon salt
6 thyme branches
4 rosemary branches
Canola oil and butter *(for browning)*

SAUCE:

1 carrot
1 onion
200 g (7 ounces) celeriac
1 tablespoon raw sugar
1/2 dl (3 1/2 tablespoons) red wine vinegar
3 dl (1 1/2 cups) hearty red wine *(not aged in oak)*
3 dl (1 1/4 cups) game or mushroom stock
2 thyme branches
4 juniper berries

ROOT VEGETABLES:

12 small potatoes
3 medium carrots
3 medium parsnips
Canola oil *(for browning)*
Butter *(for browning)*
Salt and pepper

DIRECTIONS:

1. Trim the meat. Combine the sugar, salt, thyme and rosemary and rub all over the meat. Place in a plastic bag and let rest for 3 hours at room temperature.

2. Preheat the oven to 150 °C (300 °F).

3. Brown the meat with the herbs in oil and butter. Reserve the fat in the pan for the sauce and the root vegetables.

4. Wrap the meat with the herbs in foil. Insert a meat thermometer into the thickest part. Place the foil-wrapped meat on an oven tray in the center of the oven. Reduce the temperature to 70 °C (160 °F). One kilo of room-temperature meat takes around 1 hour and 45 minutes. Turn off the oven when the meat reaches a temperature of 54 °C (130 °F).

5. Peel and slice the carrot, onion and celeriac for the sauce and brown them in the same pan as the meat.

6. Sprinkle the vegetables with sugar and let it melt. Add the remaining ingredients in the sauce and reduce until around half the original amount remains. Remove the herbs and juniper berries. For a smooth sauce, strain and reduce a little more.

7. Boil the potatoes for around 20 minutes, then drain.

8. Peel and quarter the carrots and parsnips. Brown them in oil for 6 to 7 minutes, add the butter and then transfer to an ovenproof dish along with the potatoes. Bake in the oven with the meat for around 20 minutes. Season with salt and pepper.

9. Serve with pickled chanterelles and lingonberry compote *(see recipe page 80)*.

Pickled chanterelles

4 SERVINGS

INGREDIENTS:

500 g (1 1/4 pounds) chanterelles *(or other mushrooms)*
1/2 dl (3 1/2 tablespoons) 12 % vinegar
1 dl (1/2 cup) sugar
2 dl (1 cup) water
2 teaspoons mustard seed
3 star anise

DIRECTIONS:

1. Clean the chanterelles.

2. Heat the water to boiling. Add the chanterelles and cook for around 10 seconds. Drain.

3. Heat the vinegar, sugar and water to boiling. Add the mushrooms and seasonings, reheat to boiling and immediately transfer to a sterilized jar with a screw lid. A recycled jar works just fine.

It's fantastic to be able to go into the forest and pick mushrooms, then bring them home to preserve and enjoy throughout the winter.

Swedes enjoy sweet breads and rolls with their coffee. The cinnamon roll became popular in the 1950s and is now consumed in many other countries in northern Europe and in North America. Cinnamon rolls are best when homemade, of course! Since 1999, Cinnamon Roll Day has been celebrated on October 4 every year.

Cinnamon rolls AROUND 30 ROLLS

INGREDIENTS:

1 1/4 kg (around 10 cups) all-purpose flour
5 dl (2 cups) cold milk
200 g (1 cup) sugar
200 g (7 ounces) softened butter
1 tablespoon ground cardamom
1 teaspoon salt
50 g (1 3/4 ounces) fresh yeast

1 egg, lightly beaten
Pearl sugar

FILLING:

250 g (9 ounces) almond paste
4 tablespoons (1/4 cup) ground cinnamon
250 g (9 ounces) butter

DIRECTIONS:

1. Combine the first six ingredients in the bowl of a mixer equipped with dough hooks. Crumble in the yeast. Mix slowly for around 20 minutes. Cover and let rise at room temperature for around 45 minutes.

2. Turn out the dough onto a floured board. Knead well and fold 2 or 3 times to make a compact "package" of dough. Place in a plastic bag and refrigerate while making the filling.

3. Combine the almond paste and cinnamon with a wooden spoon. Add the butter a little at a time and mix until smooth. You can knead the mixture with your hands.

4. The dough is easier to roll out when somewhat chilled. On a floured board, roll out the dough/part of the dough into a rectangle around 3–4 millimeters thick.

5. Spread the filling evenly over the dough.

6. Fold the dough into three layers. Roll it out again and roll up like a jelly roll. Cut into slices.

7. Place the slices in a muffin tin or onto a baking sheet, cover and let rise in a warm place until doubled, about one hour or slightly longer. It is important to keep them away from cold air or they won't rise.

8. Preheat the oven to 200 °C (400 °F). Brush the rolls with beaten egg and sprinkle with pearl sugar. Bake for 10–12 minutes, until golden brown.

What tastes better than freshly baked rolls and a glass of cold milk…?

This is probably the most beloved of all Swedish cakes. The original recipe was in The Princesses' Cookbook from the 1930s, written by home economist Jenny Åkerström. Swedish princesses Märtha, Margaretha and Astrid were her students, and they were especially fond of the "green cake" as she called the recipe in her book.

Three small princess cakes or one large 10–12 SERVINGS

INGREDIENTS:

4 eggs
115 g (1/2 cup + 1 tablespoon) sugar
1 teaspoon vanilla sugar or 1/2 teaspoon vanilla extract
120 g (1 cup) all-purpose flour
80 g (3 ounces) butter
2 teaspoons sugar
Marzipan sheet *(pre-rolled)*
Confectioner's sugar

FILLING:

3 dl (1 ¼ cups) whipping cream
1 batch vanilla sauce *(see Skåne apple cake, page 24)*

DIRECTIONS:

1. Preheat the oven to 200 °C (400 °F). Heat 1 liter/4 cups water to boiling in a wide saucepan.

2. Beat eggs, sugar and vanilla sugar in a bowl over the saucepan of water (a water bath). Beat until somewhat warmer than body heat, around 40–45 °C (104–113 °F). Remove from the heat and beat until cold. Use a balloon whisk if possible, as an electric mixer breaks down the air in the batter.

3. Sift the flour over the batter and fold in with a rubber scraper.

4. Pour into a cake pan and spread the batter out to the sides of the pan.

5. Bake in the center of the oven for 25–30 minutes.

6. Remove from the heat. Loosen the cake from the pan by drawing a knife between the cake and the pan. Sprinkle the top with sugar, place a sheet of baking parchment over it and then unmold the cake. Let cool completely.

7. Divide the cake horizontally into three layers of equal size. For three small cakes, cut three rounds from each layer. For one large cake, use the layers as they are.

8. Whip the cream and fold into half the vanilla sauce.

9. Spread the remaining vanilla sauce evenly over one cake layer. Top with another cake layer. Spread with a 1 1/2 cm (3/4 inch) layer of vanilla cream. Top with the final cake layer. Make a mound of the remaining vanilla cream on top.

10. Make sure that the marzipan sheet is at room temperature. Unroll. Mark the middle of the sheet and lay it on the cake, starting in the middle. Gently drape the rest of the marzipan sheet over the sides of the cake. Cut off the excess marzipan and tuck the edges under the cake. Sprinkle with confectioner's sugar and garnish with a marzipan rose.

No fruit preserves are used in a classic princess cake. A similar cake with raspberry preserves is called opera cake. When I was little, a princess cake was the best thing I knew, that symbolized "party" to me.

Rhubarb and strawberries mean summer in Sweden. Rhubarb is the symbol of early summer and strawberries mean high summer. You can't celebrate Midsummer Eve without strawberries, and they have to be Swedish strawberries, the best in the world. That is an indisputable truth. At least in Sweden. The explanation is that they grow more slowly in the north and have more time to develop their intense flavor. The best strawberries come from the northernmost part of Sweden.

Strawberry-rhubarb soup 4 SERVINGS

INGREDIENTS:

1/2 lemon
5 dl (2 1/4 cups) water
2 dl (1 cup) dry white wine, such as Sauvignon blanc
2 dl (1 cup) sugar
150 g (6 ounces) rhubarb
100 g (4 ounces) strawberries
1 pot lemon balm

DIRECTIONS:

1. Preheat the oven to 120°C (250°F).
2. Peel the zest from the lemon, removing as little pith as possible. Squeeze the juice.
3. Heat the water, wine, sugar, lemon zest and juice to boiling.
4. Cut the rhubarb into 3 cm (1 1/4 inch) sticks. Cut half the strawberries into small pieces.
5. Place the rhubarb and cut strawberries in an ovenproof dish and pour over the sugar syrup. Place in the oven for 70 minutes.
6. Remove from the oven and let cool.
7. Transfer the rhubarb to bowls with a slotted spoon. Slice the remaining strawberries and divide them among the bowls. Pour over the soup. Garnish with lemon balm leaves.

This soup also can be served ice cold. It can be cooled down faster by adding a couple of ice cubes and placing the entire dish in the refrigerator. Do not stir the rhubarb too much or it can fall apart.

RECIPE INDEX

PREVIOUS SPREAD, LEFT: IHREÅN NATURE RESERVE, SVARTHÅLL, GOTLAND.
PREVIOUS SPREAD, RIGHT: MAYPOLE, TALLBERG, DALARNA

Thanks for lending us props:
Nittsjö Keramik

www.icabokforlag.se

First edition, second printing 2013

Project leader: Ingela Holm
Photo: Bruno Ehrs
Text: Tomas Tengby
Recipes: KC Wallberg
Graphic design: Pelle Sundqvist
Photo assistant: Emil Fagander
Editor: Gunilla Wagner
English translation: Melody Favish
Repro: Italgraph Media AB
Print: Grafiche Flaminia, Italien 2013

ISBN 978-91-534-3873-1